About This Book

Title: *In Space*

Step: 4

Word Count: 188

Skills in Focus: Silent e and soft c and g

Tricky Words: stars, Earth, Mars, balls, sometimes, ago, go, into, people, fly

Ideas For Using This Book

Before Reading:

- **Comprehension:** Look at the title and cover image together. Ask readers what they know about outer space. Ask them to make a prediction about what they might learn in the book.
- **Accuracy:** Practice saying the tricky words listed on page 1.
- **Phonics:** Tell students they will read words with a soft *c* sound. The letter *c* makes the soft sound /s/ when it is followed by an *e, i,* or *y.* Read the title of the book again and ask students to find the word that has the soft *c* sound, *space.* Remind readers that the *c* is soft because it is followed by an *e.* Next, point out the pattern *a_e* in the word. Explain that this is the vowel-consonant-e pattern. The silent *e* makes the vowel before it have a long sound, saying its own name. Model how to say each sound in the word *space* slowly in isolation. Then, blend them together smoothly to say the whole word. Offer additional examples from the book, such as *shine* and *place.* Repeat with soft *g* words such as *huge* and *plunge.*

During Reading:

- Have readers point under each word as they read it.
- **Decoding:** If readers are stuck on a word, help them say each sound and blend the sounds together smoothly. After reading a sentence, you may want to point out words with silent *e,* soft *c,* and soft *g.*
- **Comprehension:** Invite readers to talk about new things they are learning about space while reading. What are they learning that they didn't know before?

After Reading:

Discuss the book. Some ideas for questions:

- What is outer space? What can you find there?
- Have you read any stories about outer space? What happened in those stories?

In Space

Text by Laura Stickney

Reading Consultant
Deborah MacPhee, PhD
Professor, School of Teaching and Learning
Illinois State University

PICTURE WINDOW BOOKS
a capstone imprint

4

Space is a big place.
It is wide and black.

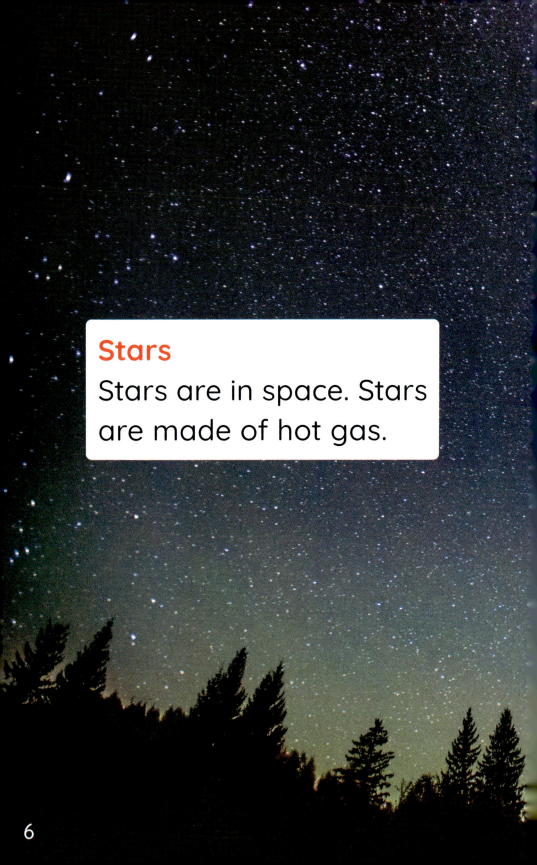

Stars

Stars are in space. Stars are made of hot gas.

To us, they shine like nice gems.

The sun is in space.
It is a huge star.

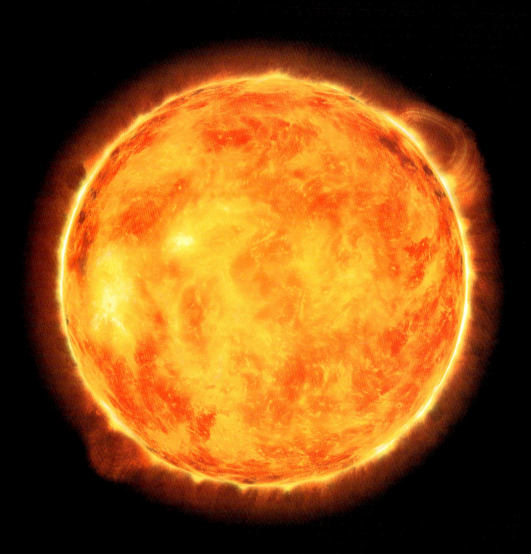

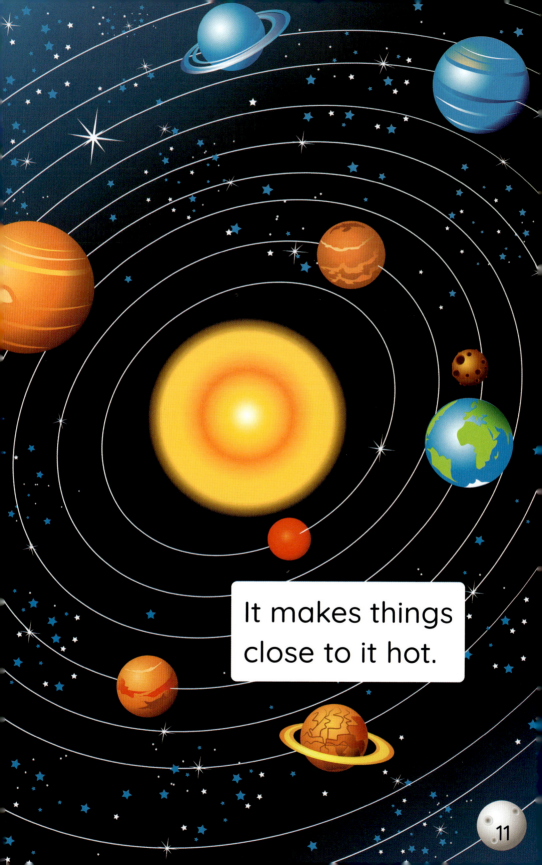

Planets

Planets are in space.

These are huge balls of rocks, gas, and sometimes ice and dust.

Earth is a planet with life! It has plants. It has lakes.

Mars is a red planet with no life. It has rocks and sand dunes.

Planets close to the sun can get hot.

Planets can have ice. Mars froze long ago.

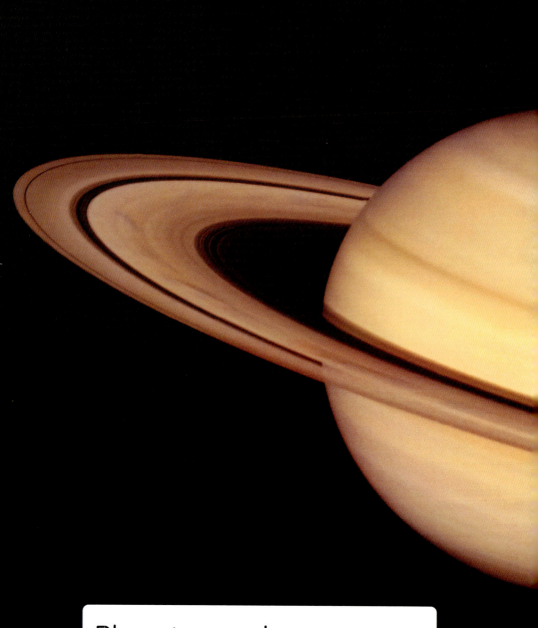

Planets can have ridges, dents, and rings.

Space Ships

Ships can fly in space. People go on long trips in space ships.

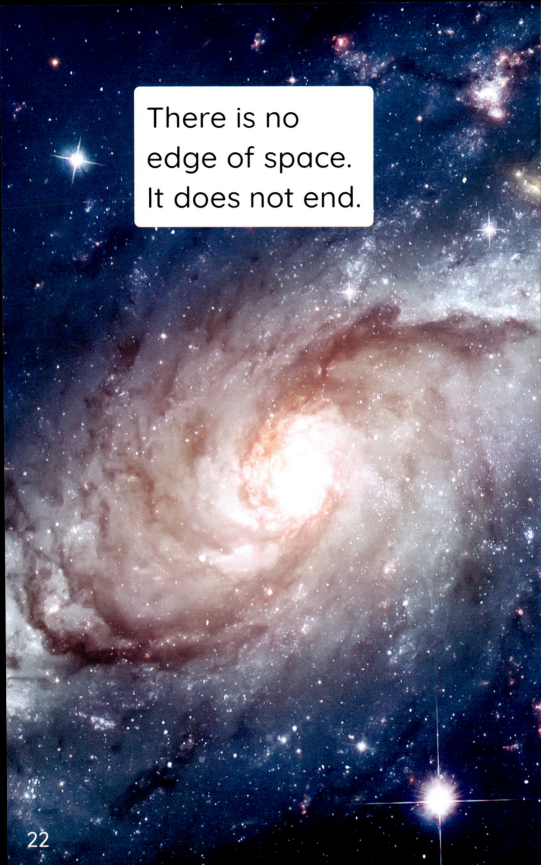

There is no edge of space. It does not end.

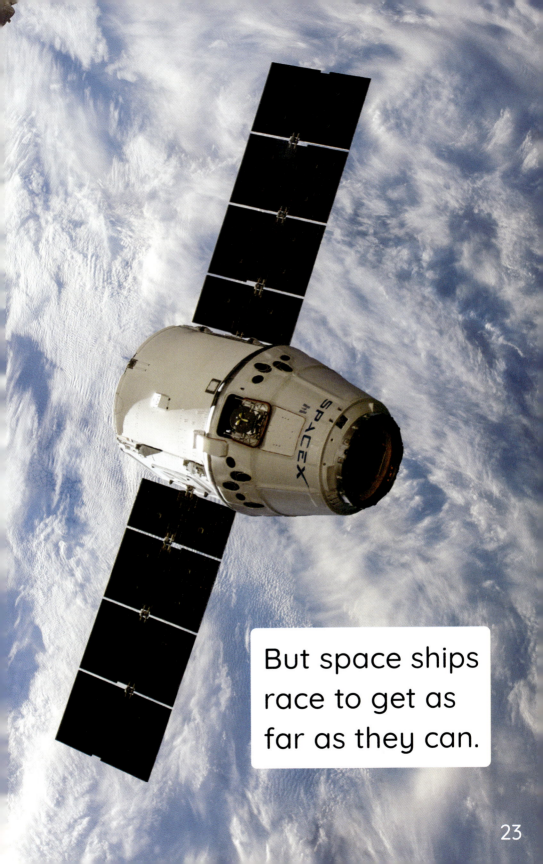

But space ships race to get as far as they can.

People on space ships can bring things back to Earth.

They bring things like rocks.

Rocks glide in space.
Ships must dodge rocks.

Rocks can strike and hit ships. Ships must brace for hits.

More Ideas:

Phonics Activity

Practicing Silent *e*, Soft *c*, and Soft *g*:

Prepare word cards with story words containing soft and hard *c* and soft and hard *g*. Distribute the cards to the readers. Have the students use a marker or highlighter to circle the *c* or *g* in each word. Then have them underline the letter following the *c* or *g* to distinguish whether the *c* or *g* in the word is soft or hard. Students can sort the cards by soft and hard sounds. Words to include:

c words:	*g* words:
• cat	• glade
• face	• page
• nice	• cage
• dance	• grade
• crack	• gel

Extended Learning Activity

What If?

Ask readers to imagine that they have discovered a new planet in outer space. What does the planet look like? What would they do on the planet? Have readers draw a picture of the planet and write a short description. Challenge them to use words with silent *e* and soft *c* and *g*.

Published by Picture Window Books, an imprint of Capstone
1710 Roe Crest Drive, North Mankato, Minnesota 56003
capstonepub.com

Copyright © 2026 by Capstone.
All rights reserved. No part of this publication may be reproduced in whole or in part, or stored in a retrieval system, or transmitted in any form or by any means, electronic, mechanical, photocopying, recording, or otherwise, without written permission of the publisher.

Library of Congress Cataloging-in-Publication Data is available on the Library of Congress website.

ISBN: 9798875227103 (hardback)
ISBN: 9798875230295 (paperback)
ISBN: 9798875230271 (eBook PDF)

Image Credits: iStock: adventtr, 12-13, Alisa Trubnikova, 4-5, dima_zel, 22, 30-31, hadzi3, 10, peepo, 2-3, standret, 6-7, themotioncloud, 16; NASA: NASA/JPL-Caltech/ASU/MSSS, 15, NASA/JSC, 1, 23; Shutterstock: 24K-Production, 28-29, Artsiom P, 18-19, 32, AstroStar, 8-9, buradaki, 26-27, canbedone, 17, Jason and Bonnie Grower, 20-21, Magnus Binnerstam, 14, Mariusz Lopusiewicz, 24-25, sababa66, 11, Triff, cover

Printed and bound in China. 6274